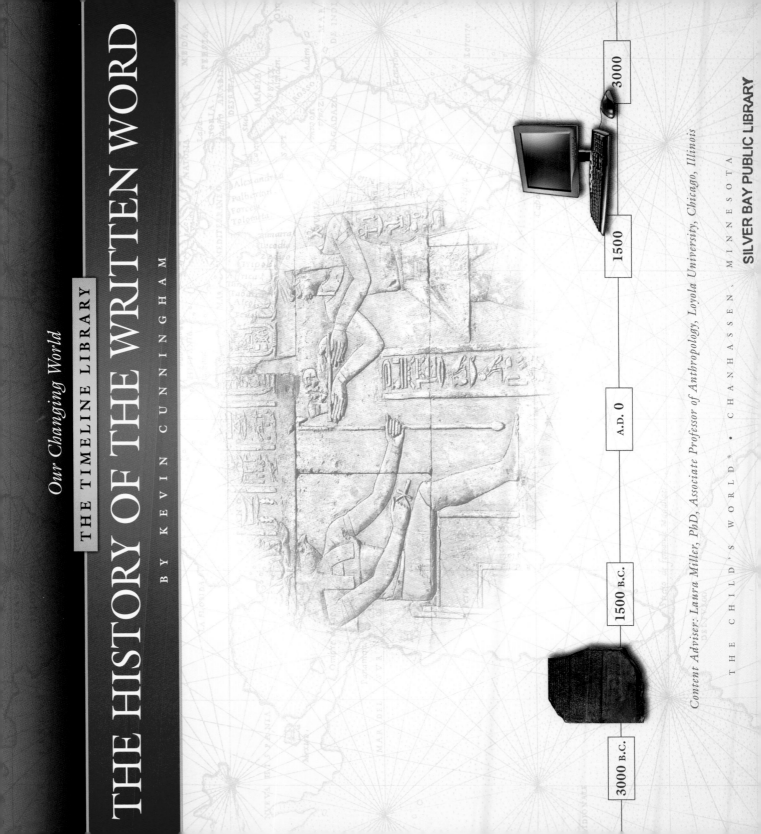

Our Changing World

THE TIMELINE LIBRARY

THE HISTORY OF THE WRITTEN WORD

BY KEVIN CUNNINGHAM

Content Adviser: Laura Miller, PhD, Associate Professor of Anthropology, Loyola University, Chicago, Illinois

THE CHILD'S WORLD · CHANHASSEN, MINNESOTA

3000 B.C.

1500 B.C.

A.D. 0

1500

3000

Published in the United States of America by The Child's World®
PO Box 326 • Chanhassen, MN 55317-0326 • 800-599-READ • www.childsworld.com

ACKNOWLEDGMENTS

The Child's World®: Mary Berendes, Publishing Director

Editorial Directions, Inc.: E. Russell Primm, Editorial Director; Katie Marsico, Associate Editor and Line Editor; Judith Shiffer, Assistant Editor; Matt Messbarger, Editorial Assistant; Susan Hindman, Copy Editor; Sarah E. De Capua, Proofreader; Peter Garnham, Olivia Nellums, Molly Symmonds, and Stephen Carl Wender, Fact Checkers; Tim Griffin/IndexServ, Indexer; Cian Loughlin O'Day, Photo Researcher; Linda S. Koutris, Photo Selector

The Design Lab: Kathleen Petelinsek, Design and Art Production

PHOTOS

Cover/frontispiece images: Corbis (main); Brand X Pictures/Punchstock (left inset); Photodisc/Punchstock (right inset).

Interior: Bettmann/Corbis: 18, 20, 24, 26; Corbis: 7 (Nik Wheeler), 10 (Sandro Vannini), 13 (Archivo Iconografico, S.A.), 16 (Araldo de Luca), 28 (Reed Kaestner); Getty Images: 5 (Thinkstock), 14 (Roger Viollet); The Granger Collection: 8, 22.

Timeline: Archivo Iconografico, S.A./Corbis: 6, 15; Corbis: 12 (Sandro Vannini), 24, 29 (Shamil Zhumatov/Reuters); Getty Images/Hulton|Archive: 10; Library of Congress: 9, 11, 19; Pictures Now: 17, 21, 22, 26.

REGISTRATION

LIBRARY OF CONGRESS CATALOGING-IN-PUBLICATION DATA
Cunningham, Kevin (Kevin H.)
The history of the written word / by Kevin Cunningham.
    p. cm. — (The timeline library)
Includes index.
ISBN 1-59296-347-1 (library bound : alk. paper)
1. Writing—History—Juvenile literature. 1. Title. II. Series.
P211.C86 2004
411'.09—dc22
                                                        2004003736

TABLE OF CONTENTS

LEAVING A NOTE

Javier finished sharpening his pencil and sat down at the desk in his bedroom. He was writing a letter to his Aunt Rosa in California. Javier lived in a different state, so he and his aunt kept in touch by mailing each other letters once a week.

When Javier was done, he logged on to his computer and typed an e-mail to his friend Carl. They were working on a science project together, and he wanted to ask Carl what time they should meet at the library. Within a few minutes, Carl wrote back and said that three o'clock would be all right.

Javier zipped his backpack and headed downstairs. Before leaving the house, he wrote a note to his mom and taped it to the refrigerator door: "Mom, I'll be home by 5:00. I'm going to study at the library." His mother was visiting with a neighbor down the street, and Javier wanted to be sure she knew where he was when she returned. Normally he would just tell her in person, but writing a note was the next best thing.

Without the written word, it would be impossible to do homework, write a letter, or read your favorite book.

Before the written word, human beings relied upon speech to communicate. Because speech is a skill that is wired into our brains, we pick it up naturally. Reading and writing, on the other hand, must be learned. Writing is a technology, similar to the wheel or the computer. We can trace it back to the earliest known civilization.

CHAPTER ONE

ANCIENT WRITING

I t's possible that art was once used as a form of communication.

Paintings of bison and rhinos from about 32,000 B.C. to 30,000 B.C. cover the cave walls at Chauvet-Pont-D'Arc in southern France.

Some cave art also includes symbols. Experts don't know if these symbols refer to objects such as water or deer, or to an idea such as "This place is safe." We also express ideas without words in the modern world, though perhaps in a different way than the cave painters did. Look at a road sign—chances are you can tell what's ahead without needing any words.

Perhaps cave art stored knowledge in the form of messages and ideas. But it wasn't a system of writing. That technology took shape in the southern regions of present-day Iraq, formerly known as Mesopotamia.

32,000–30,000 B.C.

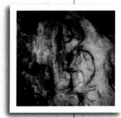

Paintings of animals cover cave walls in southern France.

2000 B.C.: CUNEIFORM

The oldest clay tablets with **pictographs** date back to 3300 B.C. and were found in the ruins of Uruk, a Mesopotamian city. Mesopotamia, the "land between the waters," was home to the first cities on earth. Traders used pictographs of products such as fish or grain to keep track of what they bought and sold. As trade increased, keeping records on clay became important. So did using symbols for numbers and names.

Hundreds of years later, the symbols began to **evolve.** The citizens of Sumer,

3300 B.C.

Mesopotamians write on clay tablets using pictographs.

The mummified remains of a prehistoric iceman found in the Alps in 1991 date back to this time.

These Sumerian ruins are located in present-day Iraq.

Sumerian cuneiform tablets such as the one shown here were useful for recording everything from laws to legends.

another Mesopotamian city, pressed symbols called **cuneiform** into clay tablets with a wedge-shaped tool. Instead of simply representing an object, cuneiform indicated a spoken sound. This allowed writing to reflect speech more closely. Stories, ideas, and laws could finally be written down.

By 2000 B.C., cuneiform had spread throughout the Middle East. When ordinary people speaking different languages needed to communicate, they wrote in cuneiform. Kings used cuneiform to brag about their greatness, although they frequently preferred to write on gold or silver tablets.

3200 B.C.

The Bronze Age begins.

King Hammurabi of Babylon ruled from 1792 B.C. until 1750 B.C. He used cuneiform to write a set of laws called the Code of Hammurabi. These laws helped him to govern his kingdom. Another famous example of cuneiform from around the same time period is *The Epic of Gilgamesh*. Written on 12 clay tablets, it is a story about the adventures of a half-god, half-human hero.

3100 B.C.: HIEROGLYPHIC WRITING

Egypt's **hieroglyphs** are the most famous form of ancient writing. The word *hieroglyph* means "sacred carving" in Greek.

Picture writing became popular in Egypt around 3100 B.C., although it appears even earlier on tools and pot-

> ### GILGAMESH
>
> FORGET SUPERMAN. GILGAMESH WAS THE WORLD'S FIRST SUPER-HERO. THOUGH A HEROIC KING OF THE CITY OF URUK, GILGAMESH ALSO MISBEHAVED SO BADLY THAT THE GODS SENT A WILD MAN NAMED ENKIDU TO TEACH HIM A LESSON. ENKIDU CHALLENGED THE KING TO AN EPIC WRESTLING MATCH. EVEN THOUGH GILGAMESH WON, THE TWO BECAME BEST FRIENDS AND SET OUT IN SEARCH OF ADVENTURE. IN THE PROCESS GILGAMESH LEARNED TO BE A BETTER PERSON AND A BETTER KING.

3100 B.C.

Hieroglyphics become popular in Egypt.

The Chinese begin mining salt in Sichuan.

tery. These ancient pictographs display mountains, stars, and other aspects of nature. Some believe the Mesopotamians gave the Egyptians the idea for writing. Mesopotamian picture writing appeared just before the first Egyptian pictographs.

Chisels and ham-

mers were needed to carve hieroglyphs in stone, but the Egyptians also used brushes and paint to write on wood, leather, and **papyrus**. Gold, ivory, and wooden writing instruments were found in King Tutankhamun's tomb.

These hieroglyphics date back to 1450 B.C. Because the animals are facing left, someone studying the hieroglyphics would start from the left and read right.

196 B.C.

Egyptians use hieroglyphics and ancient Greek to record information on the Rosetta stone.

The Romans celebrate the conquest of Spain.

Less royal writers got by with wooden tools.

Hieroglyphs are usually read right-to-left, but not always. If the animals or humans in the hieroglyphs face right, you start from the right and read left. If they're facing left, it's the reverse. Writers often drew a ring around a royal name to protect that person from injury and black magic. Hieroglyphics, like all ancient scripts, lacked punctuation.

Over time, hieroglyphs—like cuneiform symbols—began to stand for sounds. The hieroglyph sign ≈ meant "water," but it also represented a sound similar to the letter n, which is the first sound in the Egyptian word for water. The use of symbols to represent sounds proved extremely important in the next advancement of the written word—the alphabet.

THE ROSETTA STONE

Ancient people who spoke Greek conquered Egypt and began stamping out its language. Greek writing replaced hieroglyphics in the second century. Until 1799, no one was able to **decipher** the mysterious Egyptian writing. That year, French soldiers who were exploring Egypt discovered a black basalt stone near the village of Rosetta. This stone contained both ancient Greek writing and hieroglyphics. Scholars knew ancient Greek. Using the Rosetta stone to match Greek words against hieroglyphics, they worked to "decode" the hieroglyphic system.

A.D. **1799**

French soldiers discover the Rosetta stone in Egypt.

George Washington (right) dies.

CHAPTER TWO

THE ALPHABET

S ailing out of ports in Syria, Lebanon, and northern Israel, the Phoenicians were exceptional traders. They hauled goods and founded cities around the rim of the Mediterranean Sea. By 1500 B.C., the Phoenicians were looking for a method of writing that was more advanced than hieroglyphics. Cuneiform, while excellent for writing on clay, did not transfer well to the papyrus they preferred. If they were going to keep track of their far-flung business dealings, they needed a new way of writing.

1500 B.C.: THE PHOENICIAN ALPHABET

The Phoenicians probably adapted symbols from pictographs in other forms of Middle Eastern writing or from early alphabets used by peoples to the east and south.

1500 B.C.

The Phoenicians begin searching for a method of writing that is more advanced than hieroglyphics.

Queen Hatshepsut (right) rules in Egypt.

1100 B.C.

Horseback riding and the use of saddles become popular in the Middle East.

This Phoenician relief shows a man hunting lions. In addition to being famous for their alphabet, the Phoenicians were also well known for their artwork.

Daleth was a Phoenician word meaning "door." The Phoenicians took the symbol for door, Δ (note how it looks like the entrance of a tent), and made it stand for the first sound in the word *daleth*—our *d* sound.

Cuneiform worked in a similar way, but the Phoenicians needed only 22 symbols—or letters—for their writing. Users memorized the letters in order—aleph, bit, gamal, etc. Each letter represented a consonant sound in the Phoenician language.

The Phoenician alphabet was the world's first alphabet. It was widely used around the Mediterranean by about 1100 B.C. One of the earliest known inscriptions is a warning: "Beware! Behold disaster for you down here!"

1100–800 B.C.

The Phoenician alphabet is widely used around the Mediterranean.

The Phoenicians spread the alphabet on their journeys, and it worked so well that cuneiform quickly died out. Unfortunately for future scholars, the Phoenicians wrote mainly on papyrus. Their records and literature did not survive to the present day, though many stone inscriptions did.

The Phoenician alphabet was a smashing success, but it would get a helpful addition—vowels. That addition would come from the Greeks.

1100 B.C.–800 B.C.: THE GREEK ALPHABET

Sometime between 1100 B.C. and 800 B.C., the Greeks took the incomplete Phoenician alphabet and invented one of their own. They used

900 B.C.

The Greek poet Homer is born at about this time.

Someone reading a Phoenician inscription such as the one shown here would have started from the right and read left.

19 Phoenician letters to represent consonants. But the

Greeks' spoken language contained lots of vowel sounds. A

consonants-only system would have resulted in major con-

fusion. Imagine trying to read English without vowels!

The Greeks added letters for vowels, something

that had not been done before, and also for a few sounds

unique to the Greek language. Suddenly, they possessed an

incredible new technology—a written script that expressed

all of the spoken sounds of their language, in a way that

made every word distinct. An unclear sign such as "Bwr f

th dg" became a clear warning "Beware of the dog."

They used their invention to write records, letters,

laws, legal documents, poetry, plays, and philosophy

L I N E A R   B

A MYSTERIOUS SCRIPT CALLED LINEAR B WAS USED ON THE ISLAND OF CRETE AS EARLY AS 1400 B.C. SIR ARTHUR EVANS, AN ENGLISH ARCHAEOLOGIST, DISCOVERED LINEAR B IN 1900, BUT HE FAILED TO DECIPHER IT.

IN 1936, 14-YEAR-OLD MICHAEL VENTRIS HAD AN OPPORTUNITY TO VIEW ANCIENT TABLETS CONTAINING LINEAR B. WHAT THE TABLETS ACTUALLY SAID WAS UNKNOWN. VENTRIS DECIPHERED THE WRITING IN 1953. IT PROVED TO BE A SYLLABARY, A KIND OF WRITING IN WHICH THE SYMBOL REPRESENTS A SYLLABLE RATHER THAN A GROUP OF SOUNDS. AFTERWARD, VENTRIS WROTE TO THE SCHOOLTEACHER WHO HAD TAKEN HIM TO SEE THE TABLETS AND JOKINGLY INFORMED HIM THAT IT WAS "NOT QUITE THE GREEK" HE HAD LEARNED AS A STUDENT.

800 B.C.

The Greeks devise an alphabet based on the Phoenician model.

The Olmec culture thrives in Mexico.

This relief dates back to ancient Rome and shows a man writing on a tablet. The Roman alphabet is also sometimes referred to as the Latin alphabet.

on stone, pottery, papyrus, wax tablets, and lead and gold foil. They even scrawled on walls—some of the earliest known alphabet writing is Greek graffiti.

When Greek colonists moved to Italy, they took the alphabet with them. Over the centuries, it passed to the Romans. This inspired the Romans to create a 23-letter alphabet so that they could write Latin. When they set out to conquer the world, the Romans took along their system of writing.

Today, their letters are used in languages such as English, German, French, and Italian. But the Greeks get the credit for the alphabet. All of the alphabets used today, from Cherokee to Finnish, grew out of their amazing idea.

750 B.C.

Greek colonists found the city of Cumae in Italy. The Roman alphabet eventually evolves from the alphabet the Greeks bring with them.

According to legend, this is the third anniversary of the founding of Rome.

CHAPTER THREE

CHINA

Virtually every writing system used today evolved from one of two sources: the Mesopotamians or the Chinese. Not long after hieroglyphics appeared in Egypt, it is believed that Huangdi, the Yellow Emperor of China, invented writing. Systems based on Chinese writing spread to other parts of Asia, including Japan, Korea, and Vietnam.

1200 B.C.: CHINESE WRITING

Chinese is not an alphabet, but a writing system based on thousands of symbols. The oldest-known Chinese writing was recorded on tortoise shells and the shoulder bones of oxen in about 1200 B.C.

Many of the 2,500–3,000 symbols they used then can be read today. It is the only system of writing to be used continuously since its invention.

1200 B.C.

The oldest known Chinese writing is recorded on shells and bones.

According to legend, the Trojan War (right) occurs.

Emperor Shih Huang-Ti ruled China when a system of writing was developed there.

Instead of creating letters, the ancient Chinese developed **logographs.** The logographs for objects such as mountains might be based on picture writing. But the Chinese, like the Sumerians, discovered that many words could not be expressed that way.

When that happened, they borrowed a symbol from a word that sounded similar. Unfortunately, that meant a single logograph could represent many words with different meanings. In about 213 B.C., the Chinese cleared up this confusion by adding a second character to point out which meaning was intended.

The Ch'in Emperor ordered a single set of symbols to be used throughout China. This system

213 B.C.

The Chinese refine a system of writing.

Buddhism takes hold in China.

remained in use until the 1950s. In the meantime, Chinese writing grew to almost 49,000 symbols! Fortunately, readers don't need to know every single symbol to understand written Chinese.

A.D. 105: PAPER

The Chinese also invented paper. Except for actual writing systems, no invention was more important to the written word. It is believed that a Chinese official named Ts'ai Lun invented paper in A.D. 105. He soaked hemp fibers (and possibly tree bark, rags, and old fish nets) and beat the mixture into a pulp. After he drained excess water through coarse cloth, Ts'ai Lun dried the remaining fibers into a lightweight writing surface.

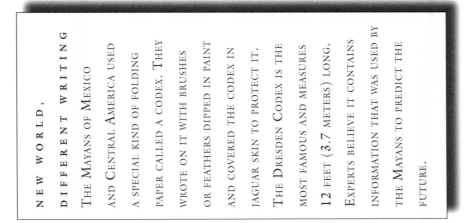

NEW WORLD, DIFFERENT WRITING

THE MAYANS OF MEXICO AND CENTRAL AMERICA USED A SPECIAL KIND OF FOLDING PAPER CALLED A CODEX. THEY WROTE ON IT WITH BRUSHES OR FEATHERS DIPPED IN PAINT AND COVERED THE CODEX IN JAGUAR SKIN TO PROTECT IT. THE DRESDEN CODEX IS THE MOST FAMOUS AND MEASURES 12 FEET (3.7 METERS) LONG. EXPERTS BELIEVE IT CONTAINS INFORMATION THAT WAS USED BY THE MAYANS TO PREDICT THE FUTURE.

A.D. 105

Ts'ai Lun invents writing paper.

Trajan (right) is emperor of the Roman Empire.

Ts'ai Lun's invention caught on. The Chinese perfected their calligraphy using a brush and paint on the paper. They previously had written on silk or other kinds of cloth.

Papermaking spread east to Korea and Japan in the sixth and seventh centuries. Soon Tibetans and Indian traders acquired the technology, and it spread west. After the year 900, Arabs used linen fibers instead of hemp or wood. They became famous for making high-quality paper.

The Mayans begin recording information on codices.

Although the Chinese initially wrote on tortoise shells and ox bones, paper proved an easier and much more efficient way of recording information.

CHAPTER FOUR

FROM PARCHMENT TO PRINTERS

While the Chinese became accustomed to paper, those to the west continued to write on ancient materials. The Romans used parchment, a surface made from animal skin (usually sheepskin). After the year 300, they replaced individually rolled-up sheets of parchment or papyrus with several sheets that were joined together to form a book. Each word was handwritten with a pen—usually a reed brush or **quill.**

When the Roman Empire collapsed in the fifth century, Christian priests and monks called scribes carried on the tradition of copying books. They usually concentrated on Bibles or other sacred works.

Meanwhile, the Arabs learned about paper. In 751, they captured a pair of Chinese papermakers. The prisoners taught the Arabs how to make the

300

Romans replace rolled-up parchment and papyrus with books.

751

The Arabs capture Chinese papermakers in Central Asia.

The Islamic empire stretches from India to North Africa.

A copy of The Diamond Sutra *is now housed at the British Museum in London, England.*

miraculous lightweight material. It soon became the rage in the Arab world. People in Egypt even stole the rags off mummies to make it.

Meanwhile, back in the east, the Chinese were carving texts into wooden blocks. After rolling ink over the carved letters, paper was stamped with the blocks. This allowed the Chinese to print several books quickly, instead of copying each by hand. *The Diamond Sutra*, the oldest known printed manuscript in the world, was printed this way in 868. The Chinese and Japanese also used the technology to make magic charms, money, and playing cards.

800s

Irish monks create the *Book of Kells* (right).

Vikings launch attacks on England.

868

The Chinese print *The Diamond Sutra.*

Paper reached Europe in the 1100s. At the same time, Europeans rediscovered reading and writing. Traders needed to know how to read and write to conduct trade. People read poetry and stories. Writers started to use everyday languages such as Italian and French instead of the Latin preferred by the Catholic Church.

1451: GUTENBERG'S PRINTING PRESS

The written word's third revolution was about to take place. German inventor Johann Gutenberg spent years working on a new method of printing called movable type. This technology used a different metal type character for each letter. A printer could move the characters to form new lines of words.

Used with other tools, movable type made European

MONKS AND BRIGHT COLORS

Monks created illuminated books with intricately drawn letters, borders, and small scenes. Occasionally they used gold or silver ink to copy an entire manuscript onto parchment that had been dyed purple. During the eighth and ninth centuries, Irish monks wrote the stunning *Book of Kells*. Now world famous, the book is considered one of Ireland's most important works of art.

Paper arrives in Europe.

Angkor Wat is built in present-day Kampuchea.

printing easier and cheaper. The Chinese invented a version of it in 1041. But they did not use it much. Keeping track of tens of thousands of different bits of type (one for each Chinese character) proved rather difficult.

Gutenberg may have printed his first work in 1451 or even earlier. No one is sure. He went broke and had to give up his equipment. But by 1456, he had printed his famous Bible.

Soon, movable type spread to Holland, Italy, and other places. Gutenberg's invention created an explosion of knowledge. Scientists and philosophers used printed books to spread their ideas. Readers rediscovered lost ideas from ancient texts. **Literacy** became necessary for success. Learning—and society—changed forever.

German inventor Johann Gutenberg (left) lived from 1397 until 1468.

1456

Johann Gutenberg, using movable type, prints the first copy of his Bible (right).

Christopher Columbus turns five years old.

CHAPTER FIVE

MASS COMMUNICATION

By the 1700s, the written word was more popular than ever. New changes in society brought it to a mass audience. Steam-powered presses appeared in the early 1800s. In 1833, a publishing company in New York called Harper & Brothers bought one of these presses to replace the horse that, walking in circles, powered their old machines. Long rolls of paper that were fed into printers were invented. Other inventions focused on new methods of holding books together.

Cheaper printing meant cheaper newspapers, books, and magazines. Readers across the United States were able to keep up with arguments over slavery and other issues. Printed pamphlets urged settlers to "Go West." During the mid- to late 1800s, business, industry, science, government, and

1833

Harper & Brothers buys a steam-powered printing press.

Great Britain abolishes slavery.

law expanded. These fields offered the best jobs, but they also required the most education. To fill these jobs, societies needed literate citizens. Governments opened public schools in the United States, Japan, much of Europe, and some European colonies. Most citizens were taught to read from a young age.

The typewriter was invented in 1867.

But not everyone believed in this new, quick way of writing. Mark Twain passed up a chance to invest in it and instead put up money for a rival machine. The typewriter caught on, the rival machine never worked, and Twain went broke.

By the early part of the 20th century, the written

Although most typewriters have since been replaced by personal computers, they were considered an amazing technological achievement during the late 1800s.

1867

The typewriter is invented.

The U.S. government buys Alaska for $7.2 million (right).

word appeared in the new entertainment craze: silent movies. Instead of hearing actors and actresses speak, the audience read written dialogue that ran across the bottom of the screen. As it turned out, movies and other visual entertainment challenged the written word's popularity. Throughout the century, and especially after 1945, many people preferred film and television to reading.

But technology related to the written word continued to advance. Photocopiers, uncommon in 1980, are now found everywhere. Computers were another huge change. In the early 1970s, typists were thrilled because word processors allowed them to correct mistakes before printing! In 1977, people began to purchase personal computers, and

WRITING TOOLS

The Romans used an early type of pencil when they wrote with sticks of lead. But in 1564, the English began to mine graphite—the "lead" in our pencils. When they inserted narrow rods of graphite into wooden holders, pencils became (and continue to be) a cheap instrument that can be used for writing and drawing. Erasers did not arrive until the late 1700s, when explorers brought rubber from South America.

1970

The first word processor is sold.

Earth Day is celebrated for the first time.

1977

The first personal computers are sold.

Star Wars becomes one of the top moneymaking films in history.

the typewriter became **obsolete** in many countries.

The written word still dominates the Internet. But companies are already developing cheap software that allows a computer to understand the human voice. When that happens, writing—by keyboard or by hand—may become unnecessary.

What we write on is also changing. In 2003, researchers announced progress on E-paper. This paper-thin plastic screen will be foldable and light. At first, it will display text, but will images be far behind? Companies already believe it'll be sewn into clothing, so you can read e-mail or the latest news on your sleeve.

With so many new technologies around the corner, the written word faces more changes and challenges. Will it vanish like cuneiform, or will it become more important than ever?

THE HEALING EFFECT OF WRITING

In September, 2003, a new study came out showing that writing could help people heal from wounds. Patients were asked to write about upsetting or stressful events in their lives for three days. A second group of patients wrote on unimportant topics. Doctors found those in the first group healed faster. Doctors now recognize that stress slows down the healing process. It may be that writing about problems or bad experiences relieves stress, allowing patients to heal more quickly.

2003

Scientists make advances in the invention of E-paper.

Forces led by U.S. troops invade Iraq (right).

From the cuneiform tablets of ancient Mesopotamia to the personal computers of modern times, the written word continues to be one of mankind's most important means of communication.

GLOSSARY

calligraphy (kuh-LIG-ruh-fee) Calligraphy is an artistic handwriting developed by the Chinese and now used in many cultures. The ancient Chinese practiced calligraphy by using a brush to apply paint to paper.

cuneiform (ku-NEE-uh-form) Cuneiform is a style of writing made with wedge-shaped tools. The people of ancient Sumer wrote in cuneiform on clay tablets.

decipher (di-SYE-fur) To decipher something is to figure out what it means. The Rosetta stone was used to decipher hieroglyphics.

evolve (i-VOLV) To evolve is to change or make progress with a task. The picture writing of ancient times began to evolve into cuneiform when people needed to start keeping written records.

hieroglyphs (HYE-ruh-glifs) Hieroglyphs are the characters used in a type of picture writing called hieroglyphics. The ancient Egyptians used hieroglyphs on their tombs, monuments, and documents.

illuminated (ih-LOO-muh-nate-uhd) Illuminated writing refers to a decorated book or manuscript. The *Book of Kells* is an example of an illuminated book.

literacy (LIT-ur-uh-see) Literacy is the ability to read or write. After Gutenberg's printing press, literacy became more widespread.

logographs (LAW-guh-grafs) Logographs are symbols used to represent entire words. The ancient Chinese wrote logographs on tortoise shells and the bones of oxen.

obsolete (ob-suh-LEET) Obsolete means no longer in use or no longer useful. Personal computers made the typewriter obsolete.

papyrus (puh-PYE-ruhss) Papyrus is a writing material made from a plant that grows along the Nile River in Egypt. The ancient Egyptians, and later the Greeks and Romans, wrote on pieces of papyrus. (Note: papyrus is not paper.)

Phoenicians (fi-NEE-shuhnz) The Phoenicians were a trading people of ancient times originally based in modern-day Syria, Lebanon, and Israel. Trade required the Phoenicians to create a way of writing better than cuneiform.

pictographs (PIK-toh-grafs) Pictographs are ancient or prehistoric drawings usually meant to represent objects. The Mesopotamians used pictographs to represent fish, grain, and other items that they traded.

quill (KWIL) A quill is a writing tool, sometimes a feather, that is dipped in ink or paint and used as a pen. The Romans used quills to write on sheets of papyrus.

FOR FURTHER INFORMATION

AT THE LIBRARY

Nonfiction

Coulter, Laurie. *Secrets in Stone: All about Mayan Hieroglyphics*. Boston: Little Brown, 2001.

Hayward, Linda. *I Am a Pencil*. Brookfield, Conn.: Millbrook, 2003.

Jeunesse, Gallimard. *The History of Making Books*. New York: Scholastic, 1996.

* Macauley, David. *The New Way Things Work*. Boston: Houghton Mifflin, 1998.

Marston, Elsa. *The Phoenicians*. New York: Benchmark, 2001.

Smith, Elizabeth Simpson. *Paper*. New York: Walker & Co., 1988.

Fiction

* McCaughrean, Geraldine, and David Parkins. *Gilgamesh the Hero*. Grand Rapids, Mich.: Eerdman's, 2003.

Books marked with a star are challenge reading material for those reading above grade level.

ON THE WEB

Visit our home page for lots of links about the written word: *http://www.childsworld.com/links.html*

Note to Parents, Teachers, and Librarians:
We routinely check our Web links to make sure they're safe, active sites—so encourage your readers to check them out!

PLACES TO VISIT OR CONTACT

Computer History Museum
1401 N. Shoreline Boulevard
Mountain View, CA 94043
650/810-1010

JAARS Alphabet Museum
Box 248
Waxhaw, NC 28173
704/843-6000

INDEX

ABOUT THE AUTHOR

KEVIN CUNNINGHAM IS AN AUTHOR AND TRAVEL WRITER WHO HAS WRITTEN FOR NEWSPAPERS, MAGAZINES, AND TRAVEL GUIDES. HE STUDIED HISTORY AND JOURNALISM AT THE UNIVERSITY OF ILLINOIS AT URBANA. HE LEARNED TO USE A TYPEWRITER JUST AS PERSONAL COMPUTERS BECAME EASY TO BUY AND USE.